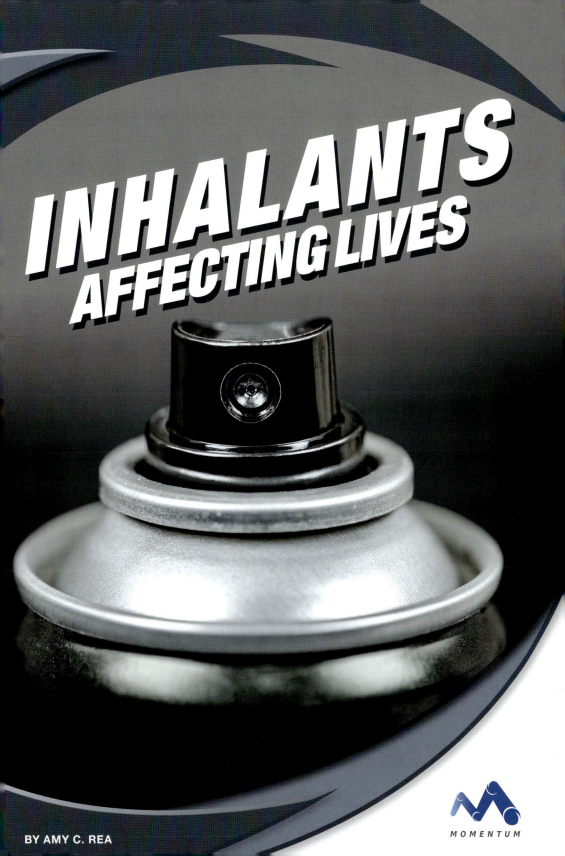

INHALANTS
AFFECTING LIVES

BY AMY C. REA

MOMENTUM

Published by The Child's World®
1980 Lookout Drive • Mankato, MN 56003-1705
800-599-READ • www.childsworld.com

ISBN 9781503844940 (Reinforced Library Binding)
ISBN 9781503846432 (Portable Document Format)
ISBN 9781503847620 (Online Multi-user eBook)
LCCN 2019957751

Printed in the United States of America

Some names and details have been changed
throughout this book to protect privacy.

CONTENTS

MOMENTUM

FAST FACTS

What They Are

► Inhalants are substances that people can inhale through their mouth or nose. These substances can cause dangerous effects on the mind.

► Street names include air blast, poppers, snappers, whippets, and laughing gas.

How They're Used

► Some people may sniff or **huff** chemicals that they have poured on a rag. Others use a "bagging" method. This means they put substances in a plastic or paper bag and breathe them in.

► Many inhalants are household items. Some people inhale them to have feelings of **euphoria**, also known as being "high."

Physical Effects

► Inhalants can cause slurred speech, dizziness, an upset stomach, vomiting, nosebleeds, loss of hearing and sense of smell, shakiness, heart damage, and weight loss. Inhalants can also cause death.

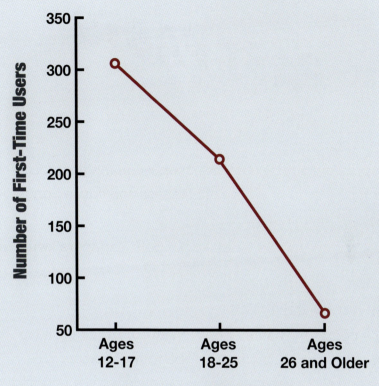

Inhalant Use by Age

Number of First-Time Users

350
300
250
200
150
100
50

Ages 12-17   Ages 18-25   Ages 26 and Older

Age of First-Time Users

"National Survey on Drug Use and Health." *SAMHSA*, 2018, samhsa.org. Accessed 6 Dec. 2019.

A 2018 national study showed that first-time use of inhalants is more common in children and teens ages 12 to 17. By age 26, the number of people who tried inhalants for the first time dropped by about 80 percent.

Mental Effects

► Inhalants can cause **hallucinations**, excitement, depression, memory loss, and irritability.

CHAPTER ONE

IT WON'T HURT ME

One Saturday night, 12-year-old Sophie was at her best friend Kate's house for a sleepover. Two other friends, Jenna and Anna, sat beside them in the downstairs basement. The girls were cozy in their pajamas and blankets. They had just finished watching a movie. It was late, and Kate's parents had gone to bed. The girls drank cans of sparkling water and passed around bowls of buttered popcorn. Music played in the background. They opened up several bottles of nail polish so they could paint each other's nails.

Then, Kate stood and said she had an idea. She remembered her mother had brought home a can of helium. Kate's mother needed it to blow up balloons for Kate's brother's birthday. Kate thought it would be fun to take turns inhaling the helium.

◄ **Some balloons contain helium. Inhaling too much helium can make someone sick.**

They could breathe some in and let it go into their lungs. It would make their voices sound funny. She went to get the can.

Sophie wasn't sure she liked that idea. She thought she had heard something about helium being dangerous. But she had also seen a famous movie star inhale helium once on TV show, and the movie star was fine. Besides, Kate said that helium was legal. Sophie thought it couldn't be that bad.

Kate came back with the can and some balloons. She filled a balloon with helium, then inhaled the helium from it. Now when Kate talked, her voice was much higher-pitched. It sounded ridiculous, and all the girls laughed.

Kate filled another balloon and passed it to Anna. Anna's voice sounded silly after she inhaled the helium, too. But after inhaling more than once, Anna had a funny look on her face. She said she felt dizzy. Kate ignored her and gave a balloon to Jenna. Jenna could not stop laughing long enough to get some words out after she inhaled the helium.

Sophie noticed that Anna looked like she did not feel well. When the balloon came to Sophie, she tried to say no. Anna and Kate started to make fun of Sophie for being scared. So, Sophie inhaled a breath full of helium and talked. Kate said Sophie's voice was the funniest one. That made Sophie less scared.

Inhaling helium can make ▶ someone's voice sound higher-pitched.

▲ **Inhaling too much helium can cause someone to pass out.**

Sophie inhaled some more. Even Anna was laughing when Sophie continued talking in her weird voice.

Then, Sophie began to feel sick. She was so dizzy that the walls looked like they were spinning. Sophie felt light-headed.

Kate was filling the balloon again. When Sophie leaned forward to take it, her vision blurred and then went black.

When Sophie woke up a few minutes later, Kate's mother was shaking Sophie and calling her name. Kate's mother said she would call a **paramedic**. When the paramedic arrived, he told Sophie she had passed out from breathing in too much helium. Sophie could see Kate, Anna, and Jenna sitting on the couch in Kate's basement. Kate was crying, and her parents stood next to her, looking very worried.

The paramedic told the girls that people thought helium was safe to inhale. But it could cause some people to faint—or even worse. People could die from inhaling helium. The paramedic said Sophie was lucky to be alive.

THE DANGERS OF HELIUM

Many people think helium is safe to inhale. But when someone inhales it, the helium takes up the space where oxygen should be in the body. Oxygen is important to keep the body functioning. Too much helium can starve the body and brain of oxygen, which leads to death. It can also damage a person's lungs or create an **embolism**. The only way to be safe is to not inhale substances at all.

CHAPTER TWO

INHALING COMPUTER DUSTER

Peter walked into his home office. The sun shone through the window. Its brightness showed Peter that there was a thin layer of dust on his desk and computer. Peter knew the computer would have dust inside it too. He needed to clean the computer so it would keep running well.

He opened a desk drawer. Last week, he had bought a pack of computer duster. But it was no longer in the drawer. He thought maybe his son, Dustin, took it. Dustin spent a lot of time working on his own computer. Peter was proud of how much Dustin knew about computers at age 14.

But when he asked Dustin about the computer duster at breakfast, Dustin would not look at him. Dustin said he and his friends had used it in a silly game. They ran around in the yard and tried to spray each other with it. Peter was annoyed.

◄ **People believe computer duster is canned air, but it contains toxic chemicals. People inhale it to get high.**

He did not like to see things wasted. He made Dustin promise not to do it again. Then, he gave Dustin some money and told him to bike to the store and buy more.

When Dustin came back from the store, he complained that his tongue hurt. Peter looked at it, but he could not see anything wrong. Peter did not notice that Dustin was hiding computer duster in his sweatshirt pocket.

The next morning, Dustin vomited. He seemed fine afterward, so Peter thought maybe it was something that Dustin had eaten. That night, Peter told Dustin to turn off his computer and clean his room. Dustin became angry and yelled at his father. He told Peter to get out of his room. Peter was shocked. Dustin never behaved like that. Peter took Dustin's laptop out of the room as punishment. Dustin slammed the door hard, then opened it and slammed it again.

The next morning, Peter was still upset with his son. He grew even more upset when Dustin didn't come to the kitchen at the normal time before school. Finally, Peter went to Dustin's room and knocked on the door. He told Dustin to get up right away. There was no answer. Peter opened the door. Dustin was sitting up against the wall. His eyes were closed. A red straw came out of his nose and a bottle of the computer duster was in his lap.

▲ **Inhaling substances can change someone's mood. It might make someone irritable or angry.**

Peter realized that Dustin had used the red straw to inhale the computer duster through his nose.

Peter shook his son's arm, and Dustin fell over on his side. Peter checked Dustin's wrist. There was no pulse. Peter grabbed his phone and dialed 911. The paramedics came quickly, but it was too late. Dustin had died from inhaling computer duster.

▲ **Inhaling substances may make someone sick to his or her stomach.**

Peter later looked around Dustin's room. He found several empty duster cans hidden under Dustin's bed and in his closet. Peter had not heard of inhalant **addiction**. He had no idea that Dustin had become addicted to inhalants.

Peter learned that people who huff often do so several times over many hours. That helps them keep the feeling of being high. But when they do that, the inhalants can quickly enter the lungs and the brain.

Peter also learned that going through several cans of duster is a warning sign of addiction. So is vomiting for no reason, and changes in behavior, such as when Dustin got angry at his dad. Dustin's sore tongue was likely due to **frostbite** from the duster. Peter wished he had known about the dangers of inhalants. Maybe then Dustin would still be alive.

GETTING HELP FOR AN ADDICTION

Trusted adults such as a parent, family member, doctor, teacher, school **counselor**, coach, or religious leader can help people find resources about addiction and give support. Someone with an inhalant addiction could benefit from working with a mental health counselor. Treatment may involve staying in a **rehab** center. That is a place where people live for days, weeks, or months while getting help with their addiction. They learn ways to avoid drugs when they return home. They also meet other people with addictions who can help each other.

CHAPTER THREE

A FRIEND GOES TOO FAR

Willow and her best friend Sarah stood in the hallway outside of their school's cafeteria. Students moved and chatted all around them. Willow played a game on her phone. Sarah sighed and said she was bored. Sarah leaned over to whisper in Willow's ear. She asked Willow to come to the bathroom with her and huff air freshener. Willow could hardly believe that Sarah had asked her to get high at school.

Over the summer, Sarah had taught Willow how to huff using a can of air freshener. Willow was amazed at how good huffing felt. They huffed other things, including whipped-cream cans. Sarah told Willow it was okay because none of these things were illegal, like "real" drugs. But she also told Willow they should not tell their parents. Sarah said parents never want them to have any fun.

◄ **People might use an air freshener to get high.**

▲ **Inhalants are often household items. Some people think these items are safe because they are not illegal, but these substances are very dangerous.**

Willow did not enjoy huffing as much anymore—she was tired of it. But it was all Sarah wanted to do, and Sarah kept finding new things to try huffing. Willow was also becoming scared of making Sarah angry. Sarah had been so fun and friendly before, but lately she could be mean. She yelled at Willow for little things. Once, Sarah was mad at Willow for suggesting they share a soda, something they used to do often. Things that never bothered Sarah before now seemed to bother her all the time. Sometimes after huffing, Sarah slurred her speech and Willow had trouble understanding her.

▲ **If people want to learn more about the dangers of inhaling, they can read about it online.**

Now Sarah wanted to huff at school. Willow said no, and Sarah got mad. But Willow didn't think it was a good idea. What if a teacher found out what they were doing? Sarah told her they were not friends anymore and walked away. Willow was not sure she could keep from crying.

That afternoon Sarah would not even sit with Willow on the bus, like she usually did. They had been best friends for eight years, but now Sarah would not even look at her.

▲ Children can tell a trusted adult if they know someone who is huffing.

Willow got home and went to the kitchen to grab a snack. Her phone buzzed when she opened the fridge. It was a text from Sarah, saying she was still angry at Willow. Willow put her phone down without answering and opened her laptop. She was not sure she believed huffing was safe and legal like Sarah had said. It was time to do some research.

After an hour of reading articles online, Willow was in tears. She had never known the dangers of huffing. Now, she was reading stories of people her age who had died or suffered brain damage after huffing too much. Willow realized she was right to be worried about her friend. She also understood all the times Sarah blew up at her were probably because of the huffing, not because she was really mad at Willow. Willow had learned that huffing can cause someone's personality to change. They can become very angry over nothing.

Willow jumped as someone knocked on her door. She heard her mom's voice, asking if she could come in. Willow froze. Her mother would see she had been crying. But maybe it was time to tell someone about Sarah's huffing and how it was changing her. Willow was scared for Sarah's safety.

Willow told her mother about what Sarah was doing. Willow's mother was as worried as she was. They read articles together on the internet. Her mother said Willow had done the right thing, even if Sarah would be mad she had told her secret. Willow's mom said she would talk to Sarah's mother. Then, she asked Willow to promise she would not huff anymore. It was a promise Willow was eager to make.

CHAPTER FOUR

STARTING AT AGE 12

When Jacob woke up, he did not know where he was. He could hear a voice that sounded far away. He realized it was his mother. She was calling—no, yelling—his name. She sounded scared.

Jacob tried to sit up, but he was so dizzy that he felt sick. The garage walls spun around him. Why was he on the floor in the garage? He wanted to tell his mother to stop yelling. But his tongue felt thick, and it was hard to get words out. Jacob's mother was trying to help him stand up. His legs felt weak, as if they could not support the weight of his body. He just wanted to lie back down and sleep.

His mother's voice grew even louder. He could not stand listening to her call his name. It made him suddenly very annoyed. He tried to tell her to be quiet, but he could not speak.

◀ **Inhaling gasoline might make someone dizzy.**

Jacob pushed against his mother's arm, which was around his shoulders. He just wanted her to leave him alone.

Jacob slowly remembered why he was in the garage. It was something he could not tell his mother. Then she would be really mad at him. Jacob had been sniffing gasoline. It was something he had been doing for four years, since he was 12 years old. He liked the way it made him feel. It made him lightheaded. While he was high, nothing bothered him. Jacob used to only sniff gas once in a while. But then he began doing it more often. Now, Jacob did it every day. He could not stop. When he was not high from sniffing gas, he missed it. It made him anxious and angry.

An ambulance pulled into the driveway. Paramedics rushed over to Jacob. They put him on a **stretcher**. He did not want to go with them, but he was too weak to fight. Then, Jacob's surroundings faded away.

When Jacob woke up, he was in a hospital room. He felt sick. A doctor stood over Jacob, looking at the set of machines next to Jacob's bed. When he saw that Jacob was awake, the doctor pulled a chair next to the bed and sat down. The doctor's voice was calm, but what he said was frightening. He said there were signs of kidney and liver damage. Treatment would be difficult.

People who sniff gasoline may find it hard to stop. ▶

▲ People who sniff inhalants may damage their bodies and have to go to the hospital.

It would be a very long time before Jacob was well again. If he continued sniffing gas, he could die.

After the doctor left, Jacob thought about what he had said. His parents came to see him, and they told him the same things the doctor had. Both of Jacob's parents looked like they had been crying. Jacob felt even worse. His mother said that the doctor had recommended a rehab program that could help him break his addiction and save his life. Jacob felt tears in his own eyes. He told his parents that he would like to try that. He would like to feel well again and not scare anyone anymore, including himself.

THINK ABOUT IT

► Why do you think some products, such as helium, are legal to get even though people can abuse them?
► Why do you think people believe inhalants are less dangerous than other drugs?
► Why do you think inhalants are more popular for young kids to use rather than adults?

GLOSSARY

addiction (uh-DIK-shun): Someone who has an addiction feels a very strong need to do or have something regularly. People who can't stop sniffing computer duster have an addiction to it.

counselor (KOWN-suh-lur): A counselor is a person who offers advice. Many people with addictions visit a counselor for help handling their addiction.

embolism (EM-buh-liz-um): An embolism is something that stops blood flow and can be dangerous. Inhaling helium can cause an embolism.

euphoria (yoo-FOR-ee-uh): Euphoria is an intense feeling of happiness. Many drugs cause someone to experience euphoria.

frostbite (FRAWST-bite): Frostbite happens when parts of the body are frozen due to exposure to cold air or certain chemicals. Inhaling computer duster can cause frostbite on the tongue and throat.

hallucinations (huh-loo-sih-NAY-shunz): Hallucinations are things that someone believes to be real, but which are not. People who sniff gasoline may have hallucinations.

huff (HUFF): To huff means to sniff or breathe something in. People might huff glue, paint, and other household items.

paramedic (par-uh-MED-ik): A paramedic is someone trained to treat medical problems, but who is not a doctor or nurse. A paramedic might save someone's life.

rehab (REE-hab): Rehab is a type of treatment for drug abuse. Most rehab centers have strict rules for patients.

stretcher (STRECH-ur): A stretcher is a special cot used to transport people to the hospital. When the boy woke up, he was on a stretcher in an ambulance.

TO LEARN MORE

BOOKS

DeCarlo, Carolyn. *Inhalant, Whippet, and Popper Abuse*. New York, NY: Rosen Publishing, 2018.

Flynn, Noa. *Inhalants & Solvents: Sniffing Disaster*. Philadelphia, PA: Mason Crest Publishers, 2012.

Sheff, David. *High: Everything You Want to Know about Drugs, Alcohol, and Addiction*. Boston, MA: Houghton Mifflin Harcourt, 2018.

WEBSITES

Visit our website for links about addiction to inhalants: **childsworld.com/links**

Note to Parents, Teachers, and Librarians: We routinely verify our Web links to make sure they are safe and active sites. So encourage your readers to check them out!

SELECTED BIBLIOGRAPHY

"Gasoline Sniffing: Effects and Dangers of Huffing." *Addiction Resource*, 22 Nov. 2019, addictionresource.com. Accessed 5 Dec. 2019.

"Inhalant Abuse Prevention." *Alliance for Consumer Education*, 2018, consumered.org. Accessed 5 Dec. 2019.

"Inhalants." *National Institute on Drug Abuse*, 16 Feb. 2017, drugabuse.com. Accessed 5 Dec. 2019.

INDEX

ABOUT THE AUTHOR

Amy C. Rea grew up in northern Minnesota and now lives in a Minneapolis suburb with her husband, two sons, and dog. She writes frequently about traveling around Minnesota.